TEXT COPYRIGHT © 2018
LOUIS ELLMAN
ALL RIGHTS RESERVED

Legal Disclaimer

The author of this book is not an attorney and makes no claim to be one. The information in this book does not create or constitute a client relationship. The materials presented in this book are based solely on the experiences of the author.

Table of Contents

Traditional Television Advertising 1
Television As An Extention Of The Radio Show 5
Radio Shows And Commercials 6
Visually Appealing And The Use Of Celebrities Tied To A Particular Demographic 7
Making The Mundane Interesting 8
Using Themes To Sell Products 10
The Host Uses It Too! 10
He Has A Show And A Product 11
Using Affiliation (Promo Code) As An Incentive 12
Taking Care of Business Twice 13
Using Celebrity Look Alike's As Subliminal Association 14
Using Music To Target People By Age 14
Using Foreign Accents To Influence People 15
Using An Official Sounding Voice 16
Using Age Related Voices To Target An Audience 17
Using Regular People To Talk About A Product 18
Using Announcers Or Print Ads To Show Off Customer Recommendations 19
Actors Who Used To Play A Certain Role In A Show Now Using That Same Persona As A SpokesPerson For A Product Or Service 20
A Couple of Ad Techniques That I Would Not Do 21
For New Customers Only? 21
Hurry Hurry Hurry! 22
The Use Of Double Branding 24
Conclusion 25

FORWARD

Thank you very much for purchasing "**METHODS OF REACHING YOUR TARGET AUDIENCE**". This book is the third in a series. The other two books from this series are "***Social Media Marketing On The Go***" and "***Writing Ad Copy People Want To Read***". Both are available on Kindle, Create Space and of course lowcostempire.com.

What the current book attempts to do is to bring to your attention many aspects of marketing that seem to go by the wayside and not ever considered. This book will ramp up your awareness level in terms of **television**, **radio** and **internet** and **social media** related ad content and different angles.. I will be showing you strategies, types of ads that you can put into place, and more importantly you will start to plainly see why certain approaches in certain venues will not work as well as other approaches. I believe that your ad copy will start to improve from the knowledge and insight you will have gained. We will examine technique after technique as to how to advertise a particular product or service. Believe me, many of these are going to be very helpful for your particular product or service.

In this book, I am also going to reveal some new concepts that I have worked with for a number of years and they will also help you to tailor your ad campaigns. Whether you are working within a marketing firm or you are working on your own and wearing many hats, this book is going to be of great help to you.

Let us now start analyzing the state of advertising and let's bring to the forefront many aspects that you may not realize or in some cases may have never even considered.

With that being said, let's do it!

Regards,

Louis

PS: If you need books on developing your company piece by piece, protecting your brand and your intellectual property, reading contracts, creating self-published books from scratch, developing your business plan, your executive summary, your elevator pitch private label marketing, Amazon Seller Central, affiliate marketing, leveraging a loyal following and more visit www.lowcostempire.com for books on all of the subjects mentioned in this paragraph. I have authored all of the books on that site and all of the books have my signature narrative style.

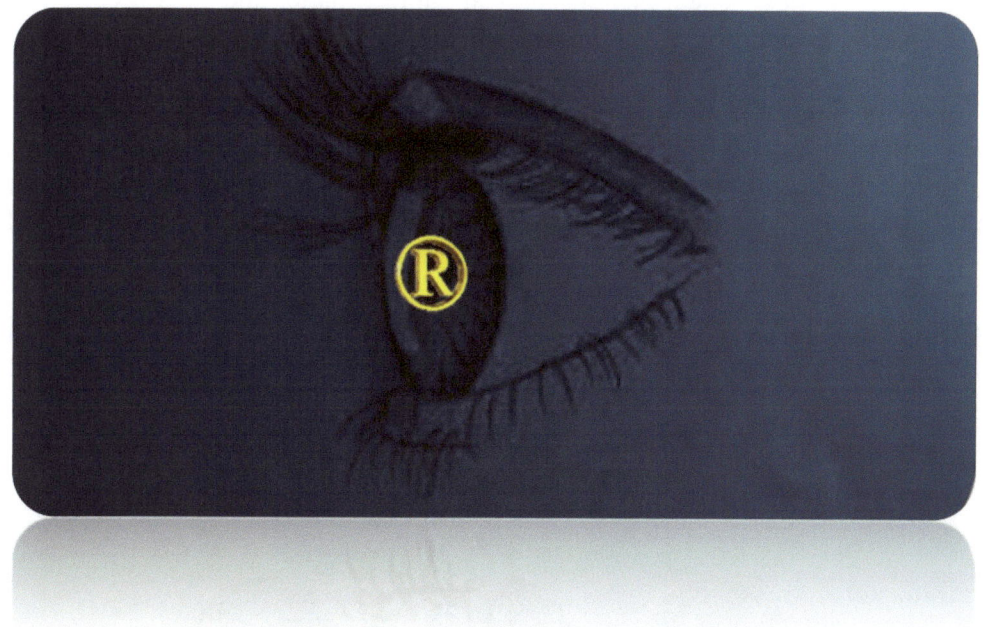

TRADITIONAL TELEVISION ADVERTISING

Traditional Television: You watch a show and then you come to a commercial break. A series of commercials play one after another. When watching television, the level of focus I would say at best is about 50-60 percent because of all of the different things you can be doing. When I look at television now, it is way more apparent that television is sometimes being used as electronic wall paper. It is there, but most often not nearly the entire focus of your attention.

The television is on, the phone rings, you now are having a conversation, you are cooking or looking at a computer at the same time and your attention is just all over the place. And, since the advent of the Internet, I would say that your attention is clearly distributed in many ways that it was not so just a few years ago. In fact, I feel that it is rare that someone's full focus is on the television show that they are watching at the time. I believe that the focus ebbs and flows and therefore when advertising comes on the television, that is a signal for many people to get up and do something else and it is used as a means to get something done while the commercials are playing out.

There are most often people in the room with you and that also lends to diversion. Commercials are also viewed by many television viewers as a unwelcome break to whatever they were watching almost like an unwelcome intrusion. In other cases, the commercial is **expected** and part of the overall event such as in football when a team takes a timeout and there is a major break in the action or in baseball when they have just ended an inning this is expected that commercials will now roll.

It all depends on the nature of the programming. Is the show currently being watched one of the following: 1) Entertainment in terms of sport, singing dance, 2) is it a documentary, serious subject matter, comical subject matter and 3) is it current events meaning a news related program. The nature of the programming is also going to affect how zoned in one is to watching a particular show. For instance, if I am watching a ball game it is something that I am going to enjoy, not stress over for the most part, and I probably will be up and down all throughout the course of the game. On the other hand, a serious documentary or a serious current event where I am learning information for the first time concerning a particular incident is going to affect my focus in a much different way.

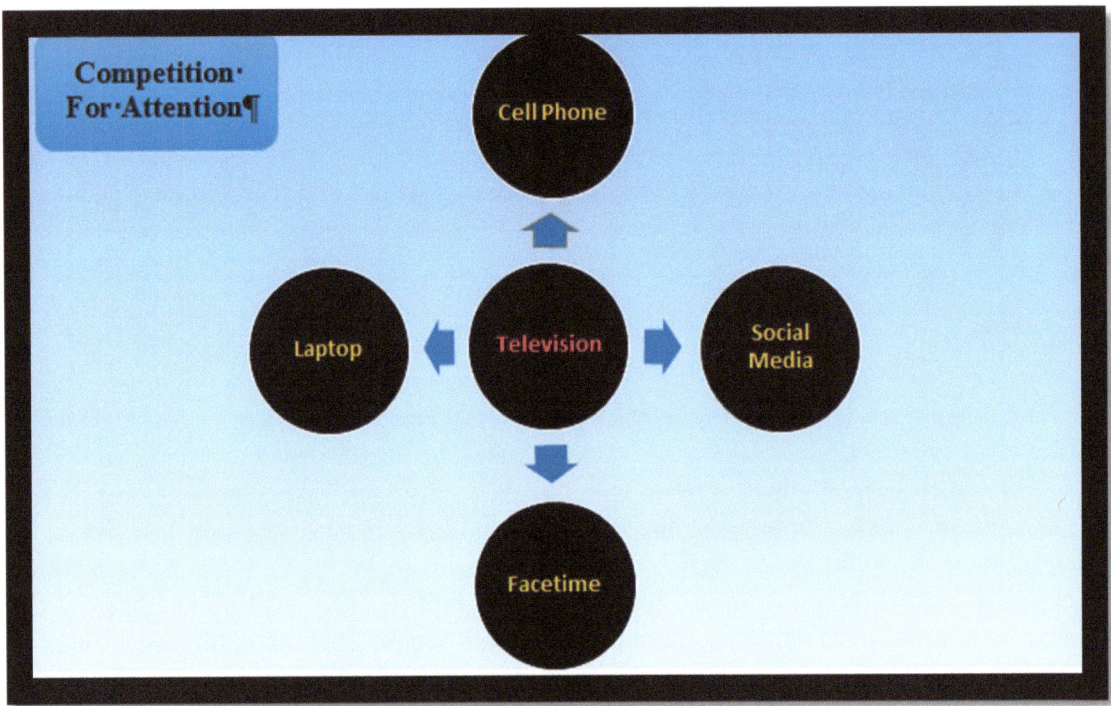

As To Commercials: When it comes to sports on the television, they really do try to match the mood of what one is watching. So, when one is watching football, you see food commercials, beer commercials, sports related commercials, body related products and that really is an attempt to match the mood and keep people within the same frame of mind so that they are that much more open to what the advertiser is attempting to convey and to sell. If I am in a great mood and having a blast watching a game and when the commercial break comes, if the first commercial that comes up is one for funeral services, it is a clash of the two moods and an individual is more likely than not to reject that current stimulus which is in direct contrast to the state of mind that he/she was in when watching the game.

A lot of people when encountering a clash, will change the channel and look around while the commercials are on in order to avoid the losing the good state of mind that they are in from enjoying the experience of the game. This is happening unconsciously but it is happening. For the most part human beings do not like to see-saw emotionally but are much more comfortable with a base line of being a comfortable state.

Going back to the serious documentary or current event that may have involved death, destruction, natural disaster and the like, the transition to a commercial about funeral services would not cause a clash and would not jar the emotional effect that one was feeling when watching that documentary of a very serious nature. In other words, death is all part of life and yes we need these services.

At other times with television advertising, the attempt to match the mood is nonexistent and I have seen the gamut on an individual commercial break. First commercial up is for a hardware item that sells for $19.99. We have all seen them. I call that "**neutral**" type advertising because **it does not affect the state of mind** that one is currently in based on the nature of the program that they are currently watching. Next up, could be for a laundry related product and again I look at that as neutral advertising and I believe that **neutral like ads** can be used at any time because they are non-controversial and do not make the mood of an individual fluctuate in any major way.

These tend to be things that are part of daily life that serve to enhance our daily life and we want to know about them and like seeing new products that are in the neutral category. Next commercial has to do with erectile problems for men and depending on the guy, he is going to have a reaction which will either be "thank God that is not me" and/or "I too am experiencing that." They are targeting a huge and diverse audience and they reckon that within that huge diversity of viewers, a fair number will be men that very well may be suffering from the effects of erectile problems. Your next commercial involves a heart drug that then ends with a variety of stated side effects that could be life threatening if you are to take the drug.

So, for that commercial sequence, they started you off with a benign set of commercials that do not cause any emotional reaction and then migrated into the more serious subject matter that definitely would affect the mood of the individual if they in fact sat through and viewed the commercial. In contrast, if I happen to be watching a medical related subject matter type show that is discussing new break troughs in medicine, then the erectile and heart drug commercial will not be that much of a spike if any, concerning the state of mind. You would have already been placed in that state by the program relating to the new medical break troughs. You are more likely to focus on the nature of the ailment in the commercial and the nature of the proposed cure when in that particular state when watching that set of commercials. This is in contrast to being in a state having **NOTHING** to do with that subject matter and then being asked to **switch gears** so to speak in order to focus on two medical oriented commercials.

NEUTRAL RELATED COMMERCIALS

In my mind, commercials that do not cause any major fluctuation in emotion, nor attempt to subliminally affect you politically are the following: Beauty, soap, make-up, food items, basic clothing items, sports related drinks, exercise equipment, natural health products, house related products such as laundry, mops, vacuum related and other mundane everyday necessary products that everyone needs and is all part of life. Those commercials are what they are and hopefully they are not politicized. I feel that these "**neutral related commercials**" are the commercials that are most likely to hit home.

Commercials that target millennials and teens could miss the mark on television simply because as a demographic, they most likely are watching a device of some sort and most probably have head phones. Sitting in the same room with headphones on, they barely notice what is going on "**television wise**" and when a commercial surfaces, unless they are truly watching the show and then stay with the targeted commercial programming, I am not sure how successful the commercial targeting is. I am going to guess that television commercial target advertising for kids, teens and young adults is still successful, but not nearly as successful as when I was a kid. As each commercial came on I would scream out that I wanted my mother to buy that particular toy or game for me.

Commercials that attempt to subliminally affect you **politically** or **socially** and send a subliminal message are some but not all: car commercials, financial commercials, drug commercials, electronic cell phone commercials, trendy food chains, and the like attempt to indoctrinate toward a specific political bent opposed to straight up advertising where the product and its merits are everything. If they think (the advertisers that is) that people do not recognize this whether it is television, radio or internet based they are mistaken. It is very obvious and it does turn some people off.

I feel that **neutral advertising is the best form** and goes to the heart of the matter **without manipulation**. If you have a good product or service and can show that within the structure of your commercials then that is very valuable.

So when dealing with television at this point, we are for the most part dealing with a scenario whereby the focus is not that heavy and if the commercials are in contrast to the state of mind produced by the nature of the commercial segment the commercial could 1) force a person to reject or tune out, 2) cause a person to temporarily change the channel or 3) unconsciously reject being yanked out of the state of mind they were comfortable in when watching the current show. You cannot please everyone all of the time and that is true for sure, but, if we are conscious as to the programming being aired and the commercials being aired we can create *a more seamless* advertising track when going on commercial breaks.

With television, another phenomenon that occurs is a person who has the television on and is somewhat paying attention while they could be simultaneously watching something on YouTube. It is very possible that while there are commercials on the television, a person will simultaneous be seeing those 5 second and "Skip" type commercials while watching YouTube so the competition to get one's attention in order to sell a product is more difficult than ever.

Not to mention the fact that to watch programming on a phone and/or tablet requires starring at the device most probably with headphones and the proximity of the screen eats up one's attention. This is in contrast to sitting a number of feet away from a television screen with no headphones and nothing hindering the ability to still hear and see the programming. Either way, traditional television has a lot of competition to contend with. Traditional television is no longer the center of attention. That is gone.

TELEVISION AS AN EXTENTION OF THE RADIO SHOW

When television first started, the advertisers had more of a captive audience because it you were in the middle of watching a show, there was much more gravity and continuity as to how people watched a show. They would tend to not miss a moment and many shows were a national event. By national event, I remember as a kid hearing tonight the Brady Bunch is on or tonight the Partridge Family is on and there was full attention to the shows that I feel is rare today. When I was very young, most of America on a Sunday night were tuned into Ed Sullivan. People today are diverted, modes of stimuli in terms of communications are many, children are more independent and often are in their own zone watching their own shows or entertainment and the family all sitting in the main room and all watching the same thing is **NOT** what we have now.

A FAMILY EVENT NO MORE

Early television was an extension of the Radio Show and when it first surfaced, it was in a way the Radio Shows coming to visual life. No longer did one listen and use their imagination in order to paint the picture but now they saw their heroes on a screen and it was mesmerizing for those early television watchers. Advertising in the early days was very neutral focused advertising and it was very effective in selling products and growing brands. Everyday items to enhance one's life were the method of the day and they were effective at creating brand loyalty and not causing mental shifts out of the zone created by the show being watched. Television was a family event and today it is just one more medium used to be entertained and to watch the news.

Finally, unlike early television, there is much more use of subliminal messaging in today's advertising and it is of course agenda driven. People do pick it up and can read between the lines. It appears to be more prevalent than ever. If I am selling something, I want my product or service to cut across all creeds, all political bents, all ages and genders. With that being said let us now move on to radio and other devices.

RADIO SHOWS AND COMMERCIALS

Radio is an interesting medium to examine regarding advertising and keeping the interest of an individual who is listening to a radio show. I believe radio is at a cross roads. People over 40, are likely to listen to a traditional radio device whether they have a car radio or a traditional AM/FM radio device. In a car, a person is a captive audience so to speak and the proximity of radio is close and therefore lends to heightened attention. If people are listening to a talk show or the news, they are likely to stick with the station and listen to the commercials that tend to be of a medical nature (a product), a financial nature (loans, financial guidance), other services that people need in business and services that assist people in everyday life such as moving companies, junk removal etc. Those type of commercials people tend to take notice of and store them in the back of their mind for when that need arises. Music related radio is more likely to have people bounce around for continuous music so that commercial breaks are an excuse to jump to another station to keep the music going.

Traditional radio I believe does well when a talk show host does the commercial and reads the ad copy. The continuity of the host transitioning over to a commercial feeds off of the audience trust of the host and their affinity of the host. In other words, if he/she thinks this is a good product then it must be a good product or else they would not lend their name to it.

The other thing that I feel that works well for both television and traditional radio are commercials by companies that have taken the time to create a character so that the audience actually enjoys the known character in the commercial. Some examples would be the **Progressive Lady** for the car insurance, the little **Geiko Gecko**, the "**Can You Hear Me Now**" phone guy, the **Mayhem** guy for insurance, the **Farmers Insurance Guy**. the "**Most Interesting Man On The Planet Guy**" for beer and so many others.

The audience gets to know the character and enjoys seeing what they are going to do in the latest commercial.

BUILDING VALUE TO THE BRAND

If the character is good and the commercials are cleaver, then those commercials take on a higher value and become **valuable branding assets** to the company that rolls out this series of commercials that make use of the character. Although it is a commercial, it serves as an additional form of entertainment that receives more attention and might provide some quick laughs **and helps to extend the brand** and heighten awareness of the product being sold. For those of you who have your own brand or work for a marketing company, *it might be a good idea for you to develop your own characters for your own products*.

Important point! Once a good television or radio ad campaign gains traction this then opens the door to print and social media type advertising because the public is now aware of the characters and just seeing them is enough to tie the visual to a brand. The Bus Ad, the print ad etc. now gets a lot more traction due to the television and radio rollout.

VISUALLY APPEALING AND THE USE OF CELEBRITIES TIED TO A PARTICULAR DEMOGRAPHIC

Younger people are more likely to bypass traditional radio and plug their smartphone into the cars speaker system and turn to a favorite internet related spot which if music related, can play 7 or 8 songs in a row before they hit a commercial and those commercials are usually cleverly targeted for the younger audience to keep them engaged. Unlike television or traditional radio, this internet related medium is **bypassing the traditional mediums** and the advertising is definitely targeted toward a younger crowd and certain types of commercials relating to medical, business and financial are **less likely** to be aired. For this group, entertainment, beauty, clothing and food related spots are more likely to be targeted for this group during a commercial break before transitioning into another solid block of uninterrupted music. One advantage that "Internet Related Radio" has is that not only can you hear the commercials but depending on the device, they can be **visually appealing** and the visual aspect helps especially if it involves a **celebrity** that that particular age group follows and that group as a whole really likes. The combination of internet related radio, ability to both hear and see and the use of **stars and celebrities** to help sell products and push entertainment all work to keep the younger audience engaged.

MAKING THE MUNDANE INTERESTING

So, when it comes to advertising, you have to be aware of all of the techniques that are being used when one is attempting to establish a brand. Let us examine 1800gotJunk.com. What they have done is to take a mundane subject "**junk removal**" and totally attach and establish a different feel and perception change. What do you think of when you hear the words junk removal? Be honest, you probably think dirty, grimey, stinky, heavy, physically demanding, guys who tell you half the story as to price, etc. What 1800gotjunk does on their radio commercials is to change the perception of junk removal and make it something professional and clean and trusting and safe and finally efficient and cost effective.

1. Establishment of a character. They introduced a character who is the crew leader for one of the supposed crews from 1800gotjunk. He has energy in his voice, he wants to please, he is courteous, he talks of their nice uniforms, he says "You just have to point" and it is done while you hear a "**Bewitched**" like effect indicating that the junk in question is gone as if by magic!

2. In each commercial he sometimes talks directly to the commercial audience while at other times, he talks to a supposed client in the commercial and interacts with them showing how smoothly the process works and how happy the clients are by having them giddy with giggly like laughter each time a junk item is removed after they simply point to it. No grimy, stinky, heavy but rather just ease, efficiency and peace.

3. Each successive commercial further moves to establish the brand, increasing the brand recognition, character recognition, "tune to brand" recognition and

they have changed the perception of junk removal to something no different than furniture delivery.

4. Finally, along with the crew chief with the pleasant, energetic voice, we have a nice melody that interweaves whistling along with the melody all adding to the mental image of the happy employee worker bees all so willing and happy to do your bidding for their very fair and affordable fees. They also create a competitive edge by offering their service until 12:00 midnight Monday-Friday as well as weekends so that you do not have to miss work to take advantage of their great service.

5. In effect, they have cleverly changed the perception of junk. They have established a good feeling to the commercial and it is very unlikely that someone would be turned off or annoyed because of the lack of résistance that is built into the business model. They are there to help, not to argue and they are there to make you happy and make you feel that you got exactly what they promised and you were left with a great feeling! A very well thought out commercial strategy that will go a long way at growing this franchise. In an era of franchises where each business is the result of a business model, the structure and perception of the company can be a make or break.

FIRMLY ESTABLISHED

6. Once the character and business has been firmly established, print ads and short radio ads with just a hint of the commercial will be **almost as effective** as the **original full length commercial**. That is the advantage of the brand recognition having kicked in and shorter commercials are now used in order to keep the company in the forefront of the consciousness of the listener while they have a chance to save a bit of advertising fee money. The hard repetitive work along with a great string of good and fun commercials now allows 1800gotjunk to use the short bursts featuring the crew chief and whistling tune to stay in the public eye.

INSTANT BRAND RECOGNITION

7. By developing the brand in the way in which they went about their business, they now have created additional **Intellectual Property Assets**. Besides their Trademark, they most probably have filed a Sound Mark for the Jingle and might have even filed for Copyright Protection concerning the musical piece. Flo who is protected by the "**Progressive Insurance**" people also have created a character which lends to instant Brand recognition, enhanced Intellectual Property and I have seen much promo merchandise that shows Flo from key chains to calendars and other items that make us think of Flo and Progressive the moment we see her. Character/song/brand bundling only helps to enhance the net worth of the asset and enhances the overall value of the company. Character development vs. straight commercials that just talk about a product or service I feel will at the end of the day lend to extending the brand more effectively than flat, plain old straight up advertising.

USING THEMES TO SELL PRODUCTS

WORD MATCHING IN ADVERTISING
THE OLD TIMERS DAY AND OLD NAVY

So every year the New York Yankees hold an Old Timers Day event before the regular game in order to celebrate the stars of yesteryear. This year, one of the main sponsors for the Old Timers Day is **Old Navy** clothing. Old Timer - Old Navy. Simple **word match** for **similarity** and **familiarity**. I do wonder how many beer companies take advantage of the name *The Milwaukie Brewers* and tie that into their beer commercials. How many airline companies take advantage of the baseball term ***ROUND TRIPPER*** (homerun) or terms of a particular genre where you can work off the terminology and work in a commercial that is cleaver and a play on words. How about the talk show host Rush Limbaugh who regularly pushes a company called **Rush Tax Advisors**. They have nothing to do with him other than they happen to share the same name to their company. You also have Mike Gallagher and one of his advertisers is **Gallagher's Steak House**. Look at the genre that you work within. What key terms, expressions and jargon of your industry can you play off of and incorporate into your ad campaign?

THE HOST USES IT TOO!

So now we have another effective advertising technique and I aptly named this section "They Use It too"! In this scenario, the host of a radio show or news show of some kind when doing a commercial for a particular product tells the audience that they have used the product or service as well. They talk highly about the product and this serves to foster credibility especially if the talk show host, guest or celebrity, has a good following and the individual already has a good reputation. Taking ownership of the product and pushing the product means that you are vouching for the product. You are giving it **a thumbs up** and that goes a long way at helping people to try the new product or service for the first time. Examples of people that "use it too" would be Joe Piscopo who tells everyone he loves and uses the "My Pillow" pillow. Other talk show hosts tell how they have used certain pain relief products. and other ex radio host John Gambling who used to talk highly about the aluminum house siding company that did such a great job for him.

HE HAS A SHOW AND A PRODUCT

Moving forward, this particular model means everything you do and push is you! Whether you have your own show, podcast, blog etc. you get the chance to show yourself off 24/7. You offer helpful advice. helpful informative shows or blog material ? Every aspect of your show. podcast or blog is all you. What better way to really get yourself out there and develop credibility. Right off the bat, I can think of **Jerry Hickey of "Invite Health"** who does a radio show on health related topics and sells his products. Another example would be Josh Gilinsky the "**Financial Quarterback**" who does a show on wealth creation and functions as a financial planner.

Another one that comes to mind it **Dotty Hermann** who is Chairman of **Douglas Elliman** who is a high end real estate company. She does a very informative radio show (**Eye On Real Estate**) and of course pushing her services for selling real estate for her would be clients. Anyone who has credibility and some experience can capitalize on this type of business model and make it work for you. This is your opportunity to become very creative in your advertising. working your advertising spots in all throughout your show. Offering certain deals and gifts if they are to engage you for an appointment stemming from the show or blog. Giving incentives for people to listen to you every week because of the value you provide. That value equals credibility and that credibility will equal referrals and business. Remember, you can do a blog, you can do a Podcast and you can do a show where you record yourself and put it on You Tube as a channel or Facebook. This is your chance to go live so to speak and not depend on others exclusively to push your products and services. For those of you who can't afford radio spots you can create your own radio show. Look up Blogtalkradio.com, iheart.com and other venues where people can hear your shows and advertisements.

USING AFFILIATION (PROMO CODE) AS AN INCENTIVE

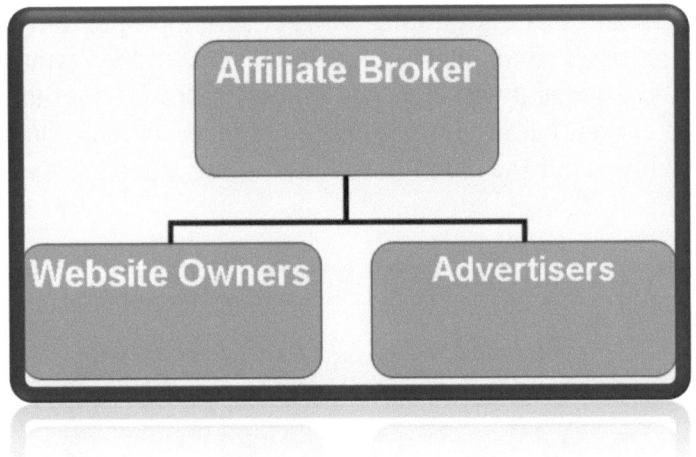

This is something that works very well. You have either a radio, television or internet related ad going. Let us say that a radio or television ad has a spokesman who says go to www.abccompany/Lastnameofhost. The "**Lastnameofhost**" part is the affiliate part of the ad. In some cases, the spokesman (usually a radio host) uses his/her name in order to assist the advertiser in accessing where the sales come from. Depending on the hours **that the ad was aired** and **the host involved**, they can get an accurate view of where the advertising was most fruitful. In other cases, the "**last name of host**" portion is an indicator to go to a landing page that gives the customer a sale or discount of some type.

That landing page is specific to that radio or television host and in some cases, as an affiliate, the host can make a percentage of the sales that are brought in from the people that went to his/her particular landing page. This is one way to encourage a host to push a product by providing them with the affiliate option as a great incentive to talk up the product and persuade people to try that product.

Another consideration are affiliate brokers like **Link Share**, **Commission Junction**, **ShareASale** and the like. In conjunction with a radio, television or internet related ad campaign, you can place your company and your products and/or service on these affiliate broker platform and then *thousands of people* can use your banners on their website that take the prospective customer over to the page or specific product or service on your website.

Those people who place the banners of the affiliate on their site will make a commission if people purchase goods/services stemming from those banners. So, when advertising your goods or services, affiliation provides an incentive for others you will never meet to nevertheless push your products and services as well. It also provides an exponential way for you the advertiser to expand your reach.

TAKING CARE OF BUSINESS TWICE

Here is yet another angle to spread the word and take care of business at the same time. So you place your ad on the radio, TV or Internet and within that ad, you ask that they call a toll free number to receive some valuable info or a gift of some kind. This method serves two purposes:

1. One, it enables you to access the ad in terms of how it draws people and based on the times that the ad was aired, which time frame was most effective?

2. By collecting people's email, you are now creating a valuable asset (mailing list) that can be used again and again to push your products and services. The more you run the advertisement, the larger the email list should grow. That list, is **targeted** and **specific** to the area or *genre* that you sell your product or service in. This is in contrast to just having a huge list without those on the list having been specifically targeted.

3. If you place your ad in different regions of the country then you have the chance to see how the ad has performed in different regions of the country or for that matter of the world. You are also collecting emails from separate regions whereby items can then be targeted to people of different regions that make sense for that region, Meaning, I don't want to sell winter coats to those living in Arizona.

USING CELEBRITY LOOK ALIKE'S AS SUBLIMINAL ASSOCIATION

Here is another technique that I personally would not use but nevertheless, here it is. There are times when a popular figure is used either **overtly** or **subliminally** in order to "**cash in**" so to speak on a celebrity. Sometimes it is done subliminally whereby they make no mention of the fact that that guy or gal looks just like let us say Obama or Trump but it is meant to cause an unconscious association and signal to the watcher of the advertisement that this individual is someone that we are in tune with. If you trust him/her trust us and this is all going on subliminally. Then you have the use of a celebrity and the look-a-like in this scenario is using the look-a-like role in a comedic manner and simply having fun while selling the product. If you do this at all, I highly recommend the comedic method and have fun doing so.

USING MUSIC TO TARGET PEOPLE BY AGE

In this particular scenario, period music is used to target a particular age group. The music helps to create a mood and to place one back in the nostalgic mindset of their youth. Using period music when the target group was young, hopeful, happy, energetic and the advertiser hopes that this feel good frame of mind then carries over and helps to associate their product with that good positive feeling!

It also serves a purpose of subliminally saying to the target that we understand you. We know where you have come from. We are on the same page as you. Our product is wanted and liked by the people of your era. We are all in a club together. We know what makes you tick and want our products to be in sync with your mind set. We get it, we get you and we want to serve you

USING FOREIGN ACCENTS TO INFLUENCE PEOPLE

So, here we are with another way to influence your prospective customers. When using foreign accents, lets start with the perspective of the American audience. I am really beginning to believe that Americans are a sucker for an accent. Let's go through some of them.

The **English accent** is used as a means to convey authority, credibility, refinement. When it is used in a comedic way, it is usually over the top and Monte Python like. The advertiser hopes to attach an aire of superiority in the quality and distinction of the product. We are who we are because of our high standards, our quality and the public's learned expectations as to our brand. Car commercials, banking and real estate or hotel related ads are just a few of the ways that the English accent is used to create that feeling of wealth, quality, high standards and all of the other ways one can describe *crème de la crème*.

The **romance languages**. Accents that stem from Italian, French and Spanish language voiceovers or actors serve a different purpose. The use of these accents serve to spur feelings of romance, relationships, love, memories of being in love, sex, sexiness, the good life, carefree, leisure, culture, cuisine, atmosphere, wine, spirits, frame of mind, day dreaming, and other mood enhancing descriptions. These type of commercials usually are effective for hotels, vacations, wines, get always, beach, tours, sexy clothing, high end cuisine and so much more. Use accents to your advantage where you feel that they can emotionally effect your audience as to how they view and feel emotionally relating to your product.

USING AN OFFICIAL SOUNDING VOICE

Here is another technique that people will use on television, radio and home grown ad campaigns. Using an official sounding voice lends to immediate credibility, immediate sense of urgency, and a sense that what is being offered is credible and what is being claimed is credible. Will an official sounding voice work for everything? No, I don't believe that it does. For example, how would an official sounding voice or personality go over for advertisements about clowns for parties, diapers, McDonalds or Popeye's Fried Chicken? I think it would come over as very silly. Where I think it works very well would be **Security**, **Medical**, **Legal** and **Education** based scenarios.

Then there is one more way that an official sounding voice is used and that is mocking officialdom. I am sure that you recognize the mocking official voice where they are using the officialdom to create *a ridiculous urgency and gravity* to get to Dunkin Donuts right away to get that Mocha Chocolate coffee that is only on sale today, or the car salesman that tells you that the prices are going up starting tomorrow and the mocking official voice is telling you that this is your **last chance** and **last warning**! The official voice, both serious and mocking, is an effective selling technique and should be considered for the right scenario.

USING AGE RELATED VOICES TO TARGET AN AUDIENCE

This is another effective means to target a particular audience. For example, an elderly gentlemen telling you that a particular drug was helping him, or how great a particular insurance company or medical insurance company is. His voice, identifying his age, is lending credibility that the service he is talking about can be trusted, the company will do what they say they will do. This voice is telling others of this age group that he trusts the company and therefore it must be good. His reassuring voice and tone letting the target audience know that he is on the same page as them, going through the same scenarios as them, has the same aches and pains as them and therefore is subliminally acting as an advocate for them. The elderly sounding female voice can be just as effective in fostering the "**trust this company**" theme based on audience trust of the spokesperson. The spokesperson become a "**iconic**" representation of what an elderly person is in America and for those people it is recognizable and embraced. The brotherhood and sisterhood of older Americans have a very tight bond. This bond responds to those who come across as sincere, confident and a tone that says trust me I have your back.

Younger voices pushing products or services serve the same dynamic. He/she is one of us. The age related voice is telling a group of teenagers or young adults about a new movie, show, phone app, brand of clothing, food item and on and on. Younger people hearing a voice or seeing a younger shill for a company makes the connection that the advertiser is looking for.

Just as the elderly audience would not take serious a youthful sounding person pushing a product or service to them, a young audience is just as likely to dismiss the elderly sounding personality as a total disconnect, a has been, not hip, you are old and we are not listening unless the situation is a product/service being pushed by an older person who is speaking to a younger crowd in the role of a grandmother or grandfather. Even the grandpa and grandma ploy may not work either. It is very possible that they are likely to feel that you are not one of us, you are old and we are not listening. So, we can see how targeting an audience based on a particular age demographic is an important and heavily used method of selling a product or service. If you use this method, listen to a lot of voices and look at a lot of personalities before you choose the one to represent you. Make sure it is a good fit.

USING REGULAR PEOPLE TO TALK ABOUT A PRODUCT

I like this method to target an audience but it can be hit or miss. Usually, this method will use local people to target the local audience. They are giving their opinion as to what they think of a particular product. When it is a favorable reply, it can work out really well simply because the regular guy/gal is talking from the heart and has no ulterior motive. They are simply enjoying giving their opinion about a particular brand.

Sometimes, though, I have seen this method backfire whereby a particular guy or gal either has an **unorthodox speech pattern or accent or personality** and it comes off as either funny or annoying. Just recently, I heard a commercial over and over again using this method that spoke about "Balance of Nature" a vitamin supplement and the woman went on and on about the sickness, the illness and "My Balance of Nature" and how the sickness and illness and boils and other horrors are now so much better. I am glad for her but it left one cringing.

Next, in that same commercial, a weak sounding woman comes on who sounded like she barely had enough energy to just say what she was saying. She said in a voice sounding like she was about to pass out that because of Balance of Nature, she now feels so much better and energetic. Trust me, I have no doubt that it is a really good product because I have heard so many everyday people on the commercial talk about it. For the woman with the weak voice I am glad for her that she was feeling better. I just don't know if I would have used that particular cut.

If you are using this method, I feel that you have to take the best of the lot and cut the ones that do not go smoothly. You want the audience to appreciate the local regular guy/gal but you also want them to **totally focus on the merits of the product and not be distracted** by the funny or annoying or the unorthodox character that the company decided to use on the commercial. The last thing I want is for my product to be laughed at or mocked because of the commercial. Discretion is important as to *who makes the final cut* but using local people can be very effective and add to the credibility of the company and enhance the good feelings toward the reputation of the product

USING ANNOUNCERS OR PRINT ADS
TO SHOW OFF CUSTOMER RECOMMENDATIONS

This is another interesting technique whereby an announcer on radio or television talks about or quotes *Ms. Smith from Illinois who is so happy with the product and all of her friends wanted to know just what is her new secret!* I know that you have seen these ads. *Mr. Jones had trouble just walking up his stairs but says he now walks 2 miles a day and never felt better!* Sometimes these type of ads are read by an announcr, voiceover person and sometimes a celebrity is used to quote these exciting and positive recommendations.

In ad copy or social media, I have seen these type of ads whereby you see a **cameo type photo** of the person and **right next to them you see their quote**. Regular people who anyone can identify with giving their hearty recommendation and this really goes a long way to show credibility. It shows that the public is using the product or service and they are really happy with the product or service which helps to eliminate the perceived element of risk.

Finally, in another variation of this same method, a company gets a recommendation and receives permission to have **an actor or/actress play the part of the happy recommending customer** by reading their words or paraphrasing what they said.

GENERIC, STRUCTURED AND CONTROLLED

A good example of this would be a law firm commercial whereby person after person tells us that **ABC Firm** got them a great settlement for their car accident, slip and fall or medical related accident etc. When they use this method, they usually make an announcement or put up text on the screen that the person you see is a **professional actor** if it is a TV commercial. An announcement that the people giving the recommdation are actors portraying the real people is typically revealed at the beginning or end if it is a radio show commercial.

They do this method because they feel that if the recommendations are done by professionals, that the audience will be more focused on the nature of the advertisement and will not be distracted by the diversity of looks, accents, quirks etc. They want a ***generic type structured and controlled approach*** to get their point across and to keep people locked in on the message. I think all of these methods have their place and can be utilized effectively.

ACTORS WHO USED TO PLAY A CERTAIN ROLE IN A SHOW NOW USING THAT SAME PERSONA AS A SPOKESPERSON FOR A PRODUCT OR SERVICE

This is another method of reaching an audience based on a popular character from a television show that people really liked and thus identify that actor as being from a certain vocation. Let me give you a really good example. In the late seventies, early eighties, there was a show called **The Streets of San Franciso** starring **Michael Douglas** and **Karl Malden**. They played detectives in that very popular show at that time.

When the show ended, Karl Malden used to use his tell tale old style hat and trench coat when he did his commercial for American Express Travelers Checks. The tag line of the commercial was "**Don't Leave Home Without Them**".

He was the law enforcement authority warning you that if you go on vacation to a foreign country that you should use travelers checks. He warns you about losing your wallet and having no way to recover the lost money.

What did he bring to the table with this type of ad? He was able to capitalize on the popularity of the character. No, he is not a real detective, but he was respected and accepted as if he were. When he tells you about something that can protect you, it was taken as sincere, the truth, valid, and if he is telling you to use Amercian Express Travelers Checks then people took him serious and thought of this as **solid advice**.

Not only did he do the commercials on television, but he also appeared on the side of bus ads and magazine ads with his tell tale trench coat and old style hat. Just seeing Karl Malden *one now thought of American Express*. This was a very effective ad and the use of the recognizable character was used very effectively for credibility.

A COUPLE OF AD TECHNIQUES THAT I WOULD NOT DO

FOR NEW CUSTOMERS ONLY?

What is this about? I have heard cable ads, insurance ads, vitamin ads, you name it, all saying "**OFFER FOR NEW CUSTOMERS ONLY**." In this particular situation, I have to hand it to them that at least they are up front and they let you know right off the bat what the policy is. This does not mean that it is a particularly smart move in terms of keeping your existing customers happy and feeling appreciated.

You are an existing customer. You hear that there is a great deal from a company you do business with all the time. You also find out that it is not for you only for brand new customers. You then say, don't I count? After all, I am a loyal customer! I think they are starting to take me for granted. Also, an existing customer has the feeling possibly that that they are being used. Okay, now that you got me as a customer, I am not worth your time any longer. I see. Hum...

You have to ask yourself. Did at some point you have a bunch of the company executives sitting in a room and one of the geniuses says: Hey, let's do a sale for new customers only! Yeah, that is a great idea Joe. Yes, let us publicly disrespect our existing and loyal customer base. After all, they are the ones who have made us successful. Let us kick sand in their face. What does it matter? They are just existing customers. We need to show a welcoming side for the new customers. Joe, you are a genius. Let's get this on the radio Monday morning. Sure thing!!!

SOME REMEDIES FOR THIS OVERSIGHT OF EXISTING CUSTOMERS.

1. First of all you must realize that it is most probably not intentional to try to slight the customer. What you have here are individuals that do not understand how important the existing loyal customers are. Their focus is off. I would bet for the most part they are not even conscious that what they are doing could potentially hurt them in the long run.

2. The mode of thinking that you see here stems from the top and shows an overall feel of inexperience in customer relations and perception of how the public views what they are doing.

3.   This concept of FOR NEW CUSTOMERS ONLY, also shows a "next" approach like heads of cattle where you've seen one you've seen them all. Who's next? They place no importance on the individual customer. They compile customers but they don't care about the perception of how the customer may feel once they are aware of this practice of rewarding new customers vs. nothing for existing customers. They totally don't understand that although a company is always in the mode of seeking new customers, you never ever do so at the expense of your existing customers. Your existing customers are a gift and you need to treat them like a gift and take good care of them from the first day that they are your customer to the last day they are your customer. The day that you take your existing customer base for granted is the first day of the end of your company. It is only a matter of time before the customer base gets hip to your attitude towards them and they look for friendlier pastures.

4.   If you make an offer for the new customer, make sure you do something in return for the existing customer. Give them perks and make them feel appreciated. The more appreciated your customer feels, the less likely they are to leave even if a competing service crops up that may do the same thing you do but cheaper. Make that personal connection with them. Don't compile customers. Bring them into the fold and take care of them.

HURRY HURRY HURRY!

This short chapter pertains to a sales tactic that I think ultimately hurts the reputation and good will of a company. The intensity of this type of ad varies but it stills comes across in a certain way. Let me explain. When a company puts out an ad which is usually a sale and they conclude or start off by saying "hurry before it's too late." You only have "X" number of hours or you only have until Sunday! Hurry, hurry!

This type of advertising in my opinion shows a lack of respect for both your existing customers and your would-be customers. This type of thinking shows that you feel that your customers are lemmings and you can treat them like low mentally individuals who do what they are told when they are told. It also shows the mercenary nature of the company. They are showing that they can care less about you. The only thing they care about is separating you from your money. Hurry hurry, you weak minded fool. Do what we tell you! You are stupid, you are to be manipulated.

This is a conscious attempt to create stress and insecurity that a particular item will disappear from the Earth forever unless you immediately run to the nearest store selling that item and buy. They are happy to make you feel desperate for what they are offering. I say, for those of you who do not have self respect hurry, hurry hurry. For those of you who respect yourself, who don't want to be treated like a moron, to ignore this type of company pitch.

You should take a second look at any company that deals with this type of let's create a stress and lack scenario. Are they actually sitting around in a board meeting discussing how great this approach is? You have to wonder if this is how they think about you, do you want to give them your hard earned money?

SOME REMEDIES TO DEAL WITH THE CONCEPT OF LACK ADVERTISING.

1. If you are selling a product or service, don't go down this road of disrespecting your customers. Sometimes, you have to take a step back and look at how the things you do and say, affect others or how they are perceived by the public.

2. Your advertising can certainly get the point across without treating your customers with little respect. Here is a novel idea. Why not tell your public that this offer will only be in effect for 24 hours and we at XYZ Company want you to benefit from this great offer. We urge you to take advantage of our wonderful offer and we know that when you see the results or the quality (depending whether it is a goods or service company) you will be glad that you did. Thank you for your patronage! Does that not feel a hell of a lot better than hurry, hurry hurrrrrrrrrrrrry!!!!!!

3. Who is running your advertising? Do you get the last yea or nay before that advertising goes out? You should. Do the individuals who do the advertising have respect for your customers? They should.

4. There are many ways to go about getting a result. In my experience, you want your customer to be comfortable and confident in the fact that your goods or service is reliable and that the company is one of good reputation and quality customer relations.

5. You don't want to approach customers as a one time experience. Your goal is to build a brand. Your goal is to build a relationship one by one. You want customers to come back to you again and again. You don't want to leave a bad taste or take on an attitude that the current campaign goes after people for a one time shot. No successful company survives with people who never go back. Every experience should be a positive experience between your company and your customers.

THE USE OF DOUBLE BRANDING

     The use of what I call "**Double Branding**" can be very effective for both print ads, electronic ads and all social media sites. Here we have a company in the example above "**Macy's**" with a nice advertisement pushing the viewer of the ad to go to **Macys.com**. Underneath that ad, we have the "**Chase Logo**". Obviously, these are two separate and distinct entities. The implication is that "**Chase**" likes **Macy's** and "**Chase**" being the bigger entity is giving a ***subliminal thumbs up*** to Macy's. Now, the concept of **Double Branding** obviously would need two willing participants.

     Let's now think of this same concept on a smaller scale. Let us say that I have a smaller company that wants to get major exposure for their product or service that they cannot afford at this point in time. There is a larger entity that likes the product or service of the smaller company, maybe they do business with the smaller entity and have the same overall vision. They can afford to produce that ad for the smaller client and for doing so, they can hop on so to speak as a sponsor like entity. The smaller entity pays **a certain portion of the ad** and the larger entity **fills in the gap**. The portion of the ad that the larger entity uses to push their own services can be just a mention of their company, an advertisement of their own or their company logo and their tag line. Either way, both entities are given the chance to enhance their visibility.

     This can be very useful for subsidiaries of a larger company whereby the main entity lends their credibility and visibility in order to help grow the base and patronage of that smaller entity. Whichever way you choose to take advantage of Double Branding it just might catapult a smaller less known entity into the spot light.

CONCLUSION

Now that we have examined a number of possible approaches don't be afraid to go after them. Get the customer reviews, come up with a character for your product or service, look for a voice that you can use again and again for familiarity and on and on. I gave you a lot of possible approaches. Experiment and see what takes hold. You never know. Be inventive, have fun, play with ideas for your ad campaigns. This was not a very long book but it covered a lot of ground. You would be surprised how inventive you can be especially when it involves your own product or service.

If you need any help my door is always open   You can email me at louisellman@gmail.com or phone me at 888-422-0692 Ext. 2.

Good luck with everything!!

www.ingramcontent.com/pod-product-compliance
Lightning Source LLC
Chambersburg PA
CBHW042322250526
R18347200002B/R183472PG45473CBX00005B/1